CONTENT

CAMERA EQUIPMENT

Camera: Canon 1D series, Canon 5D Mark II.
Canon lenses from 17mm to 500mm plus converters.

Each photograph displays the following exif data: Month, Time of Day, Aperture, Shutter speed, Lens, Exposure compensation and ISO.

All photographs in this book were taken from public footpaths or places with public access.

Early morning mist, Llanwenog
November 10.52 f8 1/2000 210mm +0.7 ISO 400

Looking northeast from Mwnt headland
December 13.45 f8 1/200 21mm +0.0 ISO 320

Sunset over Cardigan Island
October 18.16 f10 1/1250 70 mm -0.3 ISO 640

Foxgloves, Foel y Mwnt
June 08.37 f8 1/1000 275mm +0.3 ISO 400

❝ THE BEST PLACE TO PHOTOGRAPH THE COAST ❞

MWNT

OPPOSITE:
Mwnt headland from the coast path to Cardigan
May 11.18 f9 1/320 20mm +0.3 ISO 400

MWNT

The headland of Foel y Mwnt overlooks a secluded sandy beach, providing a setting for a great variety of photographic subjects: beautiful coastal scenery, lots of wildlife and a picturesque church.

Paths traverse and climb to the top of Foel y Mwnt (76m, 250'), where you will be rewarded with spectacular views over the beach and along the coast; there can be no better place to watch the setting sun. Cardigan Island lies to the west, while to the north and east is the panoramic sweep of Cardigan Bay.

Sheltered by the Foel is the whitewashed Church of the Holy Cross on a site where a church is said to have stood since the 6th century.

WILDLIFE

Mwnt is an excellent place for bird watching, from seabirds such as gannet, fulmar, razorbill and guillemot to chough, raven, peregrine, kestrel, red kite and buzzard on the headland. Smaller birds include stonechat, wheatear, whitethroat, linnet, meadow pipit, rock pipit, pied wagtail, swallow & house martin.

A great variety of wildflowers flourish along the coast and in the meadows around the church throughout the spring and summer. Bees, butterflies & moths are attracted to the profusion of wild flowers.

The summer months are also a good time to see and photograph bottlenose dolphins and atlantic grey seals from the headland - see Dolphins & Seals section.

Church of The Holy Cross
October 17.59 f10 1/100 40mm -1.0 ISO 640

Mwnt beach
July 11.50 f14 1/250 17 mm +0.0 ISO 500

Kestrel
October 15.43 f8 1/1000 700mm +0.3 ISO 800

Best time to visit.
Winter for sunsets over Cardigan Island.
Spring & autumn gales for dramatic waves.
Late spring and summer for wild flowers and
wildlife in general.

Access and facilities.
Car parking all year, small charge for parking
in the field above the beach. Toilets open from
Easter onwards. Small cafe and shop open
in the season. Paved path to toilets, beach
access by 139 steps only.

Owner. National Trust.

THE CEREDIGION COAST PATH

The Ceredigion coast path runs for 96 km (60 miles) along the west
coast of Wales, from Ynyslas on the River Dyfi in the north, to Cardigan
on the River Teifi in the south. From a photographic point of view it
offers a great diversity of scenery including cliffs, beaches, dunes,
estuaries and wildlife. Towns and villages are dotted along the path at
regular intervals, conveniently breaking up the path into short sections
with good access, so there is no need to carry camera gear long
distances to get good photo opportunities. Although the whole path is
worth exploring, four great places for photography have been selected
to feature in this book.

Penbryn from the coast path to Tresaith
April 14.05 f8 1/500 24mm +0.3 ISO 640

Sea cave, Penbryn
January 14.45 f8 1/125 15 mm -0.7 ISO 1000

Penbryn beach
August 14.58 f10 1/320 17mm +0.0 ISO 400

❛ THE BEST PLACE TO PHOTOGRAPH THE COAST ❜

PENBRYN & TRESAITH

OPPOSITE:
Tresaith waterfall
April 16.00 f8 1/800 17mm +0.7 ISO 400

PENBRYN

Penbryn is a long sandy beach, stretching over 1.5 km (1 mile) at low tide.

You can either walk along the tarmac road down to the beach or follow signposted footpaths through the wooded slopes of Cwm Lladron (the Robber's Valley). Although steep in places it is worth exploring; the floor of the woods are covered in ferns, with patches of wild flowers including bluebells and celandines in spring. A small stream runs along the bottom of the valley.

At the northeast end of the beach sea caves, pools and interesting rock formations in the cliffs are exposed at low tide. There are also rock pools at the southern end towards Tresaith, with rocks covered in limpets, barnacles, mussels and seaweeds. The beach has an almost tropical feel on calm sunny days, while westerly gales bring much more dramatic scenery as waves crash against cliffs and rocks.

TRESAITH

The village of Tresaith overlooks a small sandy beach. At the northeast end a waterfall tumbles over the cliffs and onto the beach below. It is accessible only at low tide and faces northwest. So it is late afternoon before the sun comes round, except in the depths of winter when it is in permanent shadow.

Please note, it is possible to get cut off by the tide at the north and south ends of both beaches, so don't forget to check tide times.

Winter's day, Penbryn
January 14.06 f10 1/320 28mm +0.3 ISO 800

Limpets, barnacles and mussels, Penbryn
June 13.45 f8 1/250 40 mm +0.0 ISO 320

Penbryn beach
June 14.46 f8 1/320 17mm +0.0 ISO 320

Best time to visit.
Penbryn beach all year round. Beach faces northwest, so it is afternoon before the sun lights up the cliffs.
Woods look at their best in spring.
Tresaith waterfall - late afternoon.

Access and facilities.
Penbryn. The National Trust car park is open all year at Llanborth Farm, about 400 metres from the beach. Toilets, cafe and shop are open in the season. There is a tarmac road down to a dropping off point and turning circle at the beach edge.
Owner. National Trust.

Tresaith. Limited free car parking at the end of the road down to the beach including disabled spaces. Toilets. Cafe and shop open in the season.

Pendinaslochtyn
May 15.50 f8 1/400 17mm -0.3 ISO 640

Herring gulls
April 19.52 f8 1/800 202 mm +0.7 ISO 640

Ynys Lochtyn
May 10.54 f14 1/160 24mm +0.7 ISO 500

" THE BEST PLACE TO PHOTOGRAPH THE COAST "

YNYS LOCHTYN

OPPOSITE:
Cardigan Bay, looking north from Ceredigion coast path, Ynys Lochtyn
May 13.19 f18 1/1800 17mm -0.3 ISO 500

YNYS LOCHTYN

Ynys Lochtyn is a rocky headland jutting out into Cardigan Bay, with steep cliffs, a natural arch, and a windswept plateau covered in wild flowers in May and June. The short grass turf is ideal feeding ground for chough and fulmars launch themselves from sheer rock ledges to glide over the sea. You may also see ravens, kestrels, auks, gannets together with smaller birds such as wheatear, linnet, meadow and rock pipits.

Bottlenose dolphins come to feed in the tide race off the headland. Watch out for grey seals in the sea below as well.

To the north lies the panoramic sweep of Cardigan Bay, while to the south there is a dramatic coastline of cliffs and beaches towards Llangrannog. Pendinaslochtyn, an Iron Age hill fort, overlooks the headland.

COAST PATH FROM LLANGRANNOG

Ynys Lochtyn is a 2.8 km (1.7 mile) walk along the Ceredigion coast path from Llangrannog. The path starts at sea level by the beach. It climbs steeply to give great views over the village of Llangrannog and the beach below, and the coastline towards Aberporth. Continuing along the path you will see a series of sandy coves and bays below, before reaching the lower slopes of Pendinaslochtyn. The main coast path continues round to the north, but you need to follow the clearly defined footpath which drops down steeply onto the headland of Ynys Lochtyn below.

Fulmar
May 14.53 f8 1/1250 500mm +0.3 ISO 640

Thrift
May 15.19 f18 1/125 17 mm +0.3 ISO 500

Chough
May 15.37 f8 1/1250 700mm +0.3 ISO 800

Best time to visit.
Late spring and early summer for wild
flowers, cliff scenery and wildlife.
August for heather and gorse in flower on
the moorland around Pendinaslochtyn.
Autumn and winter - late afternoon for low
angle of light and golden bracken.

Access and facilities.
Car parking (charged) and toilets in the
centre of Llangrannog, free car park off
B4334 in upper part of the village. Village
shop, pubs open all year round, cafes open
in season. Ynys Lochtyn is walking access
only, follow the Ceredigion coast path
north from Llangrannog, Ynys Lochtyn is
2.8 km (1.7 miles) north.

Owner. National Trust (Ynys Lochtyn and
Pendinaslochtyn).

Ynyslas dunes
May 10.20 f14 1/125 24mm +0.7 ISO 400

Sunset, Borth
January 15.40 f9 1/60 24mm +0.7 ISO 400

Marram Grass, Dyfi estuary
August 16.59 f4 1/2000 280mm +0.3 ISO 400

> # THE BEST PLACE TO PHOTOGRAPH THE COAST

BORTH & YNYSLAS

OPPOSITE:
Ynyslas beach
July 20.05 f10 1/160 24mm -0.3 ISO 400

BORTH

Borth has a three-mile stretch of sandy beach which is backed by a pebble storm beach. There are rock pools under the cliffs at the south end of the beach beyond the RNLI station and slipway.

Although some of the wooden groynes have been replaced by the new sea defences at this end of Borth there are plenty further up the beach as it extends northwards towards Ynyslas. These, and the tree stumps of the submerged forest, are good for providing silhouettes against the setting sun. The submerged forest is best viewed at low tide in the winter months and is exposed all the way along the beach from Borth to Ynyslas Turn.

YNYSLAS

To the north of Borth lie the sandy beach and dunes of Ynyslas. The sand dunes are best photographed early or late in the day to bring out the patterns of the ripples in the sand. The dunes are noted for their variety of wild flowers and orchids in the dune slacks in late spring and early summer.

The Dyfi estuary is a stopping off point for waders such as dunlin, sanderling, ringed plover, whimbrel and godwits on their migration in spring and autumn.

The beach is popular with windsurfers, surfers, and kite surfers and there are plenty of photo opportunities for action shots on windy weekends.

Submerged forest, Borth
February 17.02 f10 1/40 40mm +0.0 ISO 800

Sanderling, Ynyslas
September 09.37 f5.6 1/2000 400 mm +0.7 ISO 400

Shells
May 17.46 f10 1/500 138mm +0.7 ISO 640

Best time to visit.
All year round for sunsets, dune and
beach scenery.
Late spring and early summer for wild
flowers in the dunes.
Spring & autumn for migrating waders.
Winter for the submerged forest.

Access and facilities.
Borth. Small car park by the RNLI lifeboat
station. Roadside parking is possible
throughout the village dependent on
availability. Toilets, shops, cafes, pubs.
Ynyslas. Parking on the beach (small
charge in the summer, season ticket
available), small disabled car park
near the visitor centre. Visitor and
information centre and toilets open in
summer.

Owner. Ynyslas - the area is part of the
Dyfi National Nature Reserve managed
by the Countryside Council for Wales.

Harbout at night, Aberaeron
August 21.45 f8 2.5 sec 67mm -0.3 ISO 640

New Quay harbour
August 14.09 f8 1/200 67 mm +0.3 ISO 500

New Quay
July 08.03 f8 1/800 33mm +0.3 ISO 800

❝ THE BEST PLACE TO PHOTOGRAPH HARBOURS ❞

ABERAERON & NEW QUAY

OPPOSITE:
New Quay
October 09.04 f8 1/500 50mm -0.3 ISO 1250

ABERAERON

The architecture of Aberaeron is unique in this part of rural Wales with rows of colourful Georgian houses grouped around a stone-walled harbour. Built originally as a commercial port it is now home to pleasure boats, though some fishing boats still use the harbour.

Walking round the harbour is easy and there is a wealth of subject matter in this picturesque town. To photograph the houses and boats reflected in the water you need to visit on still days and a couple of hours either side of high tide. There are also good opportunities for night time photography with reflections of the house and street lights in the harbour.

NEW QUAY

In contrast, New Quay is built on a steep hill which slopes down to a stone quay, sheltered harbour and a sandy beach. Rows of houses overlook the harbour and a good vantage point is from the Quay itself. It is a working harbour: fishing boats regularly land catch on the Quay wall.

Unusually for towns and villages on the west coast of Wales, New Quay faces north east, so the houses catch the early morning sun. The harbour is sheltered from all wind directions except the north. For more dramatic scenes try visiting when a combination of strong northerly gales and high tides can result in waves breaking over the Quay.

Pwll Cam, Aberaeron
April 08.48 f8 1/400 28mm -0.3 ISO 400

Sunset, Aberaeron
August 20.52 f8 1/60 105 mm +1.0 ISO 640

Aberaeron harbour
August 19.25 f13 1/60 55mm -0.3 ISO 400

Best time to visit.
All year, but in both Aberaeron and New Quay boats are lifted out of the harbour for the winter months from November to around Easter.

Access and facilities.
Car parks (charged), limited street parking. Shops, excellent food served in a range of cafes, restaurants and pubs. Toilets. Aberaeron is noted for local food and craft shops.

The Three Bridges, Devils Bridge
May 12.15 f11 1/400 28mm -0.3 ISO 1000

Llyn Llygad Rheidol
August 16.18 f13 1/125 17 mm -0.3 ISO 640

The Arch
March 13.56 f9 1/1250 24mm +0.7 ISO 800

> # THE BEST PLACE TO PHOTOGRAPH THE UPLANDS

PUMLUMON AREA

OPPOSITE:
Llyn Llygad Rheidol from the summit of Pumlumon Fach
March 14.06 f9 1/500 17mm +0.3 ISO 500

DEVIL'S BRIDGE AND AREA

Devil's Bridge is famous for its spectacular waterfalls, ravines and The Three Bridges. Access to the falls and the little bridge over the river is by a turnstile and down a steep path with many steps. On the opposite side of the road is a turnstile to a shorter path to view the Three Bridges. The Vale of Rheidol Railway runs steam trains from Aberystwyth to the station at Devil's Bridge from Easter to October. Car parking in Devil's Bridge is free. There are seasonal shops, cafes and toilets.

Other attractions in the area worth a visit with a camera include The Arch which is on the B4574 Cwmystwyth road. There is free car parking in the adjacent Forestry Commission car park and there are walks through the woodland. If you leave Devil's Bridge in the opposite direction and head towards Ponterwyd on the A4120, you will come to the church of Ysbyty Cynfyn with its circular graveyard on your left.

PUMLUMON/PLYNLIMON

Pumlumon Fawr at 752 m (2,468 feet) is the highest mountain in mid Wales. Ascending from Maesnant, its windswept slopes give extensive views over the Nant-y-Moch reservoir and into the heart of the Cambrian Mountains, while Pumlumon Fach overlooks the lake of Llyn Llygad Rheidol. Capturing the sense of remoteness and solitude can be a challenge, but bright, breezy days when patches of light and shade chase across the hillsides are hard to beat.

Vale of Rheidol Railway
August 13.18 f8 1/500 24mm -0.7 ISO 1000

Waterfall, Devils Bridge
July 13.17 f8 1/500 40mm -0.3 ISO 2000

Ysbyty Cynfyn church
August 17.13 f11 1/125 17mm +0.0 ISO 400

Pumlumon summit route

Take the Nant-y-moch road from Ponterwyd. Turn right just before the reservoir and park on the verge just before the road ends at Maesnant. At the passing place at SN 773878 take the faint path on the south-west side of a small stream and head south-east up the steep hill. At SN 775875 the path meets a track which heads north-east and eventually arrives at Llyn Llygad Rheidol. (An alternative to this faint path is to join the track where it starts at SN 768874). In order to climb to the summit follow the track north-east then turn right onto a path just after crossing the Maesnant - the stream passes through a concrete sluice by the right of the track. Follow this path uphill as it heads south-east then east. Maesnant is on your right, while Pumlumon Fach rises to your left. Continue along the path in an easterly direction until it reaches the pass between Pumlumon Fach and Pumlumon Fawr. There is a steep drop down to Llyn Llygad Rheidol directly ahead so you need to turn south south-west to ascend the short distance to the summit, marked by a prominent cairn.

Note: Paths are poorly defined in places & muddy, so plan your route carefully and wear suitable footwear. Map, compass and navigation skills are required. Take warm/waterproof clothing; the summit is very exposed and there is no shelter.

LOCATION MAP

GETTING THERE

BY ROAD

The major towns, roads and railways of Ceredigion are shown on the map opposite.

The coastal locations of Mwnt, Tresaith, Penbryn and Llangrannog mentioned in this book are signposted off the A487, the main coast road. Lanes can be narrow and winding but pass through some beautiful countryside.

In the Uplands sections the Nant-y-Moch road mentioned is signposted off the A44 which passes through Ponterwyd. The mountain road to Soar y Mynydd and Abergwesyn is signposted off the B4343 in the centre of Tregaron.

BY BUS

Bus services link all the major towns and most villages. The main suppliers are Arriva, Mid Wales Travel and Richards Bros. The Cardi Bach is a summer coastal bus service which runs between Cardigan, Mwnt, Penbryn, Cwmtydu and New Quay.

BY RAIL

Arriva Trains provides a rail service linking Aberystwyth with the Midlands; it also stops at Borth station.

The Vale of Rheidol Railway runs steam trains from Aberystwyth to Devils Bridge from Easter to October.

PUBLIC TRANSPORT

Links to current bus and train services, including details of the Cardi Bach service, can be found on the Travel page at www. tourism.ceredigion.gov.uk.

Lland

A487
Aber
Fish

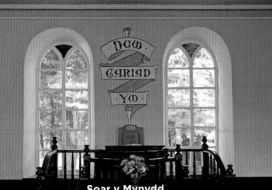

Soar y Mynydd
June 19.20 f6.3 1/15 28mm +0.3 ISO 500

Speckle ewe and lamb
May 15.19 f8 1/1000 1000 mm +0.3 ISO 1000

Soar y Mynydd
June 19.24 f8 1/100 17mm +0.0 ISO 500

> ❝ THE BEST PLACE TO PHOTOGRAPH THE UPLANDS ❞

TREGARON AREA

OPPOSITE:
Cwm Berwyn, near Tregaron
May 17.06 f10 1/200 24mm -0.3 ISO 500

TREGARON AREA

A real variety of scenery is on offer from the mountain road which leaves Tregaron for Wales' most remote chapel, Soar-y-Mynydd and then Llyn Brianne. On the way it climbs through Cwm Berwyn, a steep sided U-shaped valley, with a viewpoint looking back towards Tregaron. It emerges onto acres of sheep-grazed open moorland dotted with streams and waterfalls. Moorland birds such as wheatear, reed buntings and meadow pipits perch on roadside fence posts. The little crossroads leading to Nantymaen farm is famous for its red telephone box (photo on Useful Information page).

The simple chapel of Soar y Mynydd was built in the 1820s and stands in isolation amidst the hills near the banks of the river Camddwr. It is usually open and worth going inside. From the highly polished, wooden pews you can see painted on the wall behind the pulpit the three simple Welsh words 'Duw Cariad Yw' – God is Love, words which can be lit by the late evening sun coming through the simple stained glass windows behind you.

STRATA FLORIDA

Strata Florida or Ystrad Fflur (Vale of Flowers) lies north of Tregaron; it is signposted off the B4343 in the village of Pontrhydfendigaid. The carved archway of the west doorway is the main feature remaining of this Cistercian Abbey, together with the decorated tiled floor which is protected by a modern roof.

Moorland, Cwm Camddwr
August 17.44 f8 1/320 26mm +0.0 ISO 400

Wheatear
April 10.05 f7 1/500 700mm +0.3 ISO 1000

Strata Florida
August 15.38 f8 1/400 17mm +0.7 ISO 400

Best time to visit.
April and May for hawthorn blossom and
bluebells in Cwm Berwyn.
Late spring, summer for moorland birds.
Strata Florida - the main Archway is lit by
the sun mid afternoon onwards.
Check for opening times with CADW.

Access and facilities.
Single track road with passing places,
occasional roadside pulloffs. Car park
at Soar y Mynydd and Cwm Berwyn
viewpoint. Car parking for Strata Florida is
by the road in front of the adjacent church.
Shop, information display and toilets
available when property is open.

Speckle ewe and lambs
April 10.06 f8 1/2000 500mm +0.3 ISO 800

Lampeter
June 16.47 f10 1/250 35mm +0.0 ISO 400

Sheepdog Trials
August 17.38 f8 1/640 700mm +0.3 ISO 1000

THE BEST PLACE TO PHOTOGRAPH THE COUNTRYSIDE

OPPOSITE:
Welsh Black Cattle, Talybont
May 15.11 f8 1/640 98mm +0.0 ISO 800

LIVESTOCK AND SHOWS

The Ceredigion rural landscape consists of gently rolling hills and valleys, rising to the more open moorland of the Cambrian Mountains. Farming, especially sheep and the Welsh Black cattle, have helped to shape the present landscape.

Lambing starts early in the lowlands, but the beginning of April is the traditional start date for hill lambing. All the photos here were taken from the roadside on travels round the Aberystwyth, Devil's Bridge and Tregaron area. The Welsh Black cattle were photographed near Talybont, but there are herds scattered throughout the county.

The countryside provides the perfect backdrop for Agricultural Shows, Vintage Shows, Horse Shows, Sheepdog Trials, Trotting races and more. Visit the events page on the Ceredigion Tourism website to keep up to date with events in the county (details under Useful Information).

The County Agricultural Shows of Aberystwyth and Cardigan are held at the beginning of June and end of July respectively, with smaller shows elsewhere throughout the summer.

The Aberaeron Festival Of Welsh Ponies & Cobs is held in August with stunt displays, running of the stallions, and more.
Harness (or trotting) racing is a popular form of horse racing in Ceredigion. Races are fast and you are close to the action. There are three venues at Tan y Castell (Aberystwyth), Tregaron and Lampeter.

Trotting races at Tan y Castell, Aberystwyth
August 18.22 f7 1/2000 111mm +0.3 ISO 800

Spring
April 15.26 f9 1/1000 250mm +0.3 ISO 640

Feeding time, Rheidol Valley
April 10.03 f8 1/2000 500mm +0.0 ISO 640

Best time to visit.
Most shows are held between Easter and September.

Access and facilities.
Car parking, toilets and refreshments are normally supplied and most have an entrance fee.

Atlantic grey seal
July 09.52 f8 1/800 700mm +0.0 ISO 800

Bottlenose dolphins
August 11.21 f8 1/2500 500mm +0.3 ISO 800

Atlantic grey seal pup
October 15.47 f7 1/640 700mm +0.3 ISO 1600

> ❝ THE BEST PLACE TO PHOTOGRAPH DOLPHINS & SEALS ❞

OPPOSITE:
Bottlenose dolphin and calf
September 12.41 f8 1/500 35mm +0.0 ISO 800

BOTTLENOSE DOLPHINS

Cardigan Bay is home to a resident bottlenose dolphin population, and you don't even have to get in a boat to see and photograph them! From May to September you may spot dolphins at various locations along the Ceredigion coast including Aberystwyth, New Quay, Ynys Lochtyn, Aberporth and Mwnt. Winter sightings are much less frequent as they move offshore. Two of the best photographic locations for bottlenose dolphins are from the quay at New Quay and from the headland overlooking Mwnt Bay, where patient watching and waiting may be rewarded with spectacular acrobatic displays and high speed fish chases. Wildlife watching boat trips which run from New Quay and Cardigan are also a good way to see seabirds & seals as well as dolphins. If you do venture onto the water yourself and come across dolphins remember they are protected by law. For details on obtaining the marine code see the Useful Information section.

ATLANTIC GREY SEALS

Seals are usually seen as they pop their heads up out of the water or haul out on the rocks. They may be seen the length of the Ceredigion coast, but two of the best places to photograph them are at the Cardigan Island Coastal Farm Park, and at Mwnt, especially when there are anglers about! Although a few pups are born in Ceredigion, the main pupping beaches are further south in Pembrokeshire.

Atlantic grey seal
October 13.33 f8 1/320 500mm +0.3 ISO 1600

Bottlenose dolphins
June 09.55 f7 1/2500 500mm +1.0 ISO 640

Atlantic grey seal
October 13.02 f8 1/1000 700mm +0.3 ISO 800

Best time to visit.
Dolphins - summer months from May to
September
Seals - all year round but again summer
months are best.

Access and facilities.
New Quay. Car parks (charged), limited
street parking. Shops, cafes, restaurants
and pubs. Toilets.
Mwnt. Car park all year (charged). Toilets
open from Easter onwards. Small cafe and
shop seasonal opening.
Cardigan Island Coastal Farm Park
(Gwbert, near Cardigan). Car park,
entrance fee, toilets, shop, cafe, children's
play area. Open Easter to October. Follow
the brown road signs from Cardigan.

Red kite
December 13.51 f9 1/800 700mm -0.3 ISO 800

Red kites
March 14.52 f8 1/2000 400mm +0.3 ISO 500

Red kites following tractors
May 10.57 f9 1/1600 35mm +0.3 ISO 640

' THE BEST PLACE TO PHOTOGRAPH RED KITES '

OPPOSITE:
Red kite
March 15.23 f8 1/2000 400mm +0.7 ISO 640

BWLCH NANT YR ARIAN

The Red kites are fed daily at Bwlch Nant yr Arian. They are best photographed from the lakeside path looking across the lake to where the food is placed. The light is behind you and you can photograph the birds as they swoop in to pick up food off the ground. Good flight shots can be had when the birds wheel round overhead or fight over scraps of food on the wing.

In winter the low angle of sun lights up the underside of the kites and if you visit when snow is on the ground the light is even better, the snow acting as a giant reflector.

Also don't forget to look behind you! Birds like to perch in the trees by the path.

PHOTOGRAPHING IN THE WILD

Travel along any road through Ceredigion and you would be unlucky not to see several kites hovering over villages, farms and more remote sheep pastures looking for carrion or small mammals and birds. However, one of the better roads is the upper section of the A4120, which runs from Aberystwyth to Devil's Bridge. The coast road between Aberystwyth and Cardigan is a very good place to spot them too.

Red kites follow tractors at hay or silage making time in good numbers, providing excellent photo opportunities of birds in the wild. Also, watch out for them on the ground in fields where they feed on worms and other invertebrates.

Red kite
February 14.19 f8 1/2000 400mm +0.7 ISO 640

Red kites, Bwlch Nant yr Arian
November 15.13 f8 1/500 40 mm -0.3 ISO 1600

Red kites feeding, Bwlch Nant yr Arian
November 15.10 f8 1/2000 400mm +0.7 ISO 100

Best time to visit Bwlch Nant yr Arian.

All year round, though please note these are totally wild birds and numbers coming in to feed can vary.
In winter when the angle of sun is low to light up the underside of the birds.
Birds are fed daily at 2pm in the winter and 3pm in the summer.

Access and facilities.
Bwlch Nant yr Arian. Car park (charged). Visitor Centre with toilets, cafe and shop. Adventure play area. Picnic areas. Disabled parking and access. Footpaths round lake and hillside. There are normally bird feeders by the visitor centre.

Owner. Forestry Commission Wales.

History of the Red Kite

The story of the Welsh Red kites is one of conservation success. Once a common sight all over Britain in towns and the countryside, the red kite was persecuted to near extinction. About 100 years ago just a few pairs survived in refuges in the remote parts of the Cambrian Mountains. Since then landowners, local communities and conservation bodies (mainly the Welsh Kite Trust and the RSPB) have worked tirelessly to restore numbers and there are now several hundred pairs in Wales.

Pied Flycatcher
May 11.00 f8 1/500 1000mm +0.0 ISO 2500

Wood anemone
April 14.99 f3.5 1/500 90mm +0.3 ISO400

Blue tit
March 11.25 f8 1/2000 700mm +0.0 ISO 800

" THE BEST PLACE TO PHOTOGRAPH THE SEASONS "

SPRING

OPPOSITE:
Bluebells, Oak woods, Ynyshir
May 12.32 f10 1/50 47mm +0.0 ISO 640

RSPB YNYS-HIR

The RSPB reserve of Ynys-hir lies on the Dyfi estuary and comprises Welsh oak woodland, wet grassland and saltmarsh.

In spring, the floor of the oak woods is carpeted in flowers, notably Bluebells, Wood anemones and Celandines.

Bird song fills the air. As woodland birds such as Pied flycatchers, Common redstarts, and Wood warblers set up territories, they provide good opportunities for photography. There is also a bird feeder by the visitor centre where you can sit on a bench and photograph at close quarters a variety of birds including Chaffinch, Greenfinch, Blue tit, Great tit, Coal tit, Nuthatch, Great spotted woodpecker, and possibly Siskin.

Good places to photograph butterflies, damselflies and dragonflies are from the boardwalks that cross the reserve.

LLANERCHAERON

Set in the beautiful Aeron valley, near Aberaeron, Llanerchaeron comes alive with flowers early in the Spring. During March about seventy types of Daffodils and Narcissus come into bloom in the Walled gardens, followed in April and May by blossoming apple and pear trees. The adjacent woodlands round the car park and across the River Aeron contain, according to time of year, Snowdrops, Wood anemones, Primroses, Celandines, Ramsons and Bluebells.

Llanerchaeron is a working organic farm: as well as producing fruit, vegetables and herbs, livestock include Welsh Black cattle, Llanwenog sheep and Welsh pigs.

Daffodils
March 15.21 f11 1/100 90mm +0.3 ISO 400

Bluebell
April 14.04 f5.6 1/250 90mm +0.0 ISO 800

Apple blossom
May 14.03 f5.6 1/250 144mm +0.3 ISO 400

Best time to visit.
Flowering times vary with spring
weather but as a general guide:
Snowdrops - February.
Daffodils - late February to March.
Wood anemones - April.
Bluebells - late April to May.
Apple blossom - May.
Pied flycatchers and Common
redstarts - late April to May.

Access and facilities.
RSPB Ynys-hir. Car park. Toilets.
Visitor centre/shop. Reserve open
dawn to dusk. The visitor centre
is open daily 9am - 5pm from
April to October and 10am - 4pm
from November to March (closed
Mondays and Tuesdays).
Full details on www.rspb.org.uk.

Llanerchaeron. Car park. Shop
(gifts, farm produce, plants),
cafe and toilets are available
when property is open. Adjacent
woodland and parkland open all
year. Garden and house opening
times on the Llanerchaeron page at
www.nationaltrust.org.uk.

Furnace Falls
November 12.02 f8 1/10 40mm -0.3 ISO 400

Fly agaric
November 13.48 f6.7 1/350 400mm +0.0 ISO 400

Beech woods, Hafod
November 14.01 f6.3 1/400 373mm +0.0 ISO 800

❛THE BEST PLACE TO PHOTOGRAPH THE SEASONS❜

AUTUMN

OPPOSITE:
Bwlch Nant yr Arian
November 13.02 f10 1/250 17mm -0.7 ISO 800

BWLCH NANT YR ARIAN

Set amidst the Cambrian Mountains, time your visit for a crisp, still autumn day to photograph golden larch trees reflected in the lake. Access is easy via a short circular lakeside path. On a clear day there are good views down the Melindwr valley towards Aberystwyth from the viewpoint by the car park. You can also explore the surrounding forest and moorland on marked trails. Details of these walks are available on site.

FURNACE FALLS

Furnace Falls are located beside a large 18th century wooden water wheel in the village of Eglwysfach. They are next to the main A487 road, about 16 km (10 miles) north of Aberystwyth. For superb autumn colours, follow the minor road which leaves the main road at SN 685953. It climbs west, then south, through the deciduous woodlands which surround the falls, and then onto open moorland.

HAFOD

The Hafod Estate lies below the B4574, between Cwmystwyth and Pontrhydygroes. There is a free car park signposted on the south side of the road at SN 768736. Details of woodland and riverside walks are on the information board in the car park. The paths are steep and muddy in places but generally well marked. They will take you through a variety of deciduous and coniferous woodland, past tumbling waterfalls and over bridges across the streams.

Rhaiadr Peirian, Hafod
September 16.26 f11 1/1.7 24mm +0.0 ISO 640

Furnace
November 15.21 f14 1.0 40mm +0.0 ISO 250

Furnace
October 13.11 f9 1/50 105mm +0.0 ISO 500

Best time to visit.
All three locations as the trees turn colour,
usually from mid October to November.

Access and facilities.
Bwlch Nant yr Arian. See Red kite page.

Furnace Falls. Open access to Falls and
adjacent woodland, free parking opposite
side of A487 down a small lane on
Aberystwyth side of the bridge. Admission
to Furnace and wheel is free. For opening
times visit www.cadw.wales.gov.uk.

Hafod. Free car park, information board
showing paths.

Owners.
Furnace Falls: CADW.

Bwlch Nant yr Arian & Hafod:
Forestry Commission Wales.

Sunset, Borth
January 18.13 f4.5 1/2000 70mm +0.7 ISO 800

Morning mist, Borth and Dyfi estuary
January 9.24 f8 1/250 100mm +1.0 ISO 400

Anvil cloud, Ynyslas
September 19.36 f7 1/250 29mm +0.3 ISO 800

❝ THE BEST PLACE TO PHOTOGRAPH THE WEATHER ❞

OPPOSITE:
Shower clouds, Dyfi Estuary
April 17.47 f11 1/200 24mm +0.3 ISO 500

SUNSETS

The northern half of Ceredigion faces west so the sun sets over the sea, whereas in the south you can get fantastic sunsets as the sun drops behind the Preseli Hills. Look out for cloud formations to add interest, as in the anvil thunder cloud over the sea at Ynyslas. The Ceredigion Tide Tables list sunrise and sunset times.

WAVES

Strong onshore winds, high tides and a big ground swell combined with back lighting create ideal conditions for dramatic wave photographs.
The waves breaking over the Stone Jetty in Aberystwyth were photographed from the Prom, the low winter sun providing the back lighting and approaching storm clouds the dark sky. The Mwnt photo was taken as sunlit waves rebounded off the cliff face which was in deep shadow.

MIST AND FOG

Morning mist and fog form in low lying valleys when the air is damp and temperatures fall rapidly overnight. The photo on the Content page was taken from the A475 at Llanwenog, looking south into the Teifi valley. The Dyfi valley is also prone to mist, as in the photo above which was taken from Upper Borth.
Sea fog is common along the coast in spring and early summer when warm air from the south rides over the cold sea surface. The Aberystwyth photo was taken from the top of Constitution Hill as banks of fog drifted in off the sea.

Sea fog, Aberystwyth
March 18.22 f8 1/50 47mm +0.0 ISO 800

Waves, Mwnt beach
October 12.51 f8 1/2500 400mm -0.3 ISO 500

Waves breaking, Aberystwyth
December 13.25 f11 1/1250 200mm -0.7 ISO 50

SHOWER CLOUDS

Prevailing westerly winds bring changeable weather to the Cardigan Bay coast. Typical April showers swept up the Dyfi estuary at Ynyslas bringing heavy showers interspersed with brilliant sunshine and rainbows.

USEFUL INFORMATION

WEATHER, TIDES and SAFETY

Before setting off be sure to check the weather, tide times and that you have a map and compass if needed. Don't rely on mobile phones; reception can be patchy at best. If you are going walking, bear in mind weather conditions in West Wales can change rapidly. Be prepared, take suitable clothing and wear appropriate footwear.

When walking the Coast Path, for your own safety keep to the path, avoid the cliff edge and take extra care in windy weather.

Don't forget to protect your camera from the elements too!

Weather forecasts for Wales are available at www.metoffice.gov.uk.

Tide Tables for Ceredigion are available from local shops, newsagents and Tourist Information Centres. Included are times of sunrise and sunset.

MARINE CODE OF CONDUCT

On display on Information Boards at all launch sites in Ceredigion, the code is also available at the Boat Place, New Quay, and harbour offices. It can be downloaded from the publications page at www.cardiganbaysac.org.uk.

TOURIST INFORMATION CENTRES

Open all year except Borth and New Quay (Easter to September)

Aberystwyth TIC, Terrace Road, Aberystwyth, SY23 2AG. 01970 612125

Aberaeron TIC, The Quay, Aberaeron, SA46 0BT. 01545 570602

Cardigan TIC, Theatr Mwldan, Cardigan, SA43 2JY. 01239 613230

Borth TIC, High Street, Borth, SY24 5HY. 01970 871174

New Quay TIC, Church Street, New Quay, SA45 9NZ. 01545 560865

ORGANISATIONS

CADW: www.cadw.wales.gov.uk

Cambrian Mountains Initiative: www.cambrianmountains.co.uk

Ceredigion Coast Path: www.ceredigioncoastpath.org.uk

Ceredigion Tourism website: Events are listed, plus lots more at www.tourism.ceredigion.gov.uk

Countryside Council for Wales: www.ccw.gov.uk
(For information on Public Rights of Way, Open Access land and the Countryside Code in Wales)

Forestry Commission Wales: www.forestry.gov.uk.

National Trust: www.nationaltrust.org.uk/wales.

RSPB: www.rspb.org.uk.

Information correct at time of going to press. Errors and Omissions Excepted. Access and facilities may be subject to change and some facilities may not be available all year round. Please check before you travel.

TELEPHONE

Nid Yw'n Derbyn Arian